the local church and Pioneers

a handbook for partnership

Published by Pioneers-USA

DEAR CHURCH PARTNER,

It is a privilege to partner with you in the work of world evangelization. Pioneers is committed to building substantive and meaningful relationships with Great Commission churches. Our staff is at your disposal. One specific tool is this church partner handbook. We believe this manual will help to answer some of the most frequently asked questions. Please contact our office at any time if you have additional questions or if we can be of any further help.

More than 3,400 U.S. churches participate financially in the support and sending of missionaries through Pioneers. As you can imagine, they come with a great variety of expectations. While we cannot meet all of the needs, my prayer is that Pioneers will honor the name of Jesus Christ by effectively doing all that we can to help you connect globally.

I believe we are in the "final stretch" of the global mission endeavor. It is amazing to think that in any given week as many as 2,000 new churches are established around the world. As one of our African leaders likes to say, "This thing is getting out of control!" Together, let's make the most of the opportunities God is giving us!

Yours in His cause,

Steve Richardson

Stephen L. Richardson
President

TABLE OF CONTENTS

01 INTRODUCTION

From its beginnings in 1979, Pioneers has been a movement infused with passion and faith; a passion for God and His glory, and the expectation that He will do great things through His humble and obedient servants.

The Pioneers spirit is expressed in the oft-quoted words of William Carey, "Expect great things from God. Attempt great things for God." This dependence on God combined with outward initiative characterized Pioneers founder, Ted Fletcher. His life of faith and sacrificial obedience proved powerfully attractive as he challenged like-minded visionaries who wanted to give their lives in the cause of world evangelization.

From its inception, Pioneers has recognized that it exists to partner with local churches.

In a very real sense, Pioneers was built and designed from scratch; its architects largely a generation of youthful leaders who looked at the missionary task through new lenses. The underlying question was simply, "How do we best accomplish our God-given mandate to take the gospel to all peoples?" Structures and methods followed, with an emerging and distinctive Pioneers character.

From its inception, Pioneers has recognized that it exists to partner with local churches to see whole communities transformed by the power of the gospel of Jesus Christ. From our modest beginning in 1979, we have grown to the point where we now have ministries in 95 different countries, mobilization bases in eight locations around the world and over 200 teams seeking to obey Christ's command to make disciples of all nations.

History

In 1973, Ted Fletcher left the position of national sales manager for *The Wall Street Journal* and, with the backing of their local church, he and his wife, Peggy, stepped out in faith and founded Pioneers in 1979. That first year the new organization sent career missionaries to Nigeria and summer workers to Papua New Guinea. The goal of Pioneers has always been to avoid duplication of the work of others. We desire to share the gospel with those whom no one else is reaching.

Pioneers has continually attracted eager candidates with a passion for God and an unrelenting desire to make Christ known where people have never heard His name.

Pioneers has continually attracted eager candidates with a passion for God and an unrelenting desire to make Christ known where people had never heard His name. The growth of the movement has been a clear indication of God's blessing as we now have over 2,400 members (67% USA) and continue to see that number increase each year.

Pioneers is a combination of multiple mobilization bases. These have developed through both expansion and mergers with other organizations that joined with Pioneers. Some notable milestones in this history include the former Asia Pacific Christian Mission, South Pacific Partners, World Outreach Fellowship, Caleb Project/ACMC and Arab World Ministries. Each organization had a rich heritage and each began with a strong burden for unreached peoples.

The U.S. mobilization base relocated from its original site in northern Virginia to Orlando, Florida in 1992. In 1998, a 10,000 square foot Missionary Service Center was completed as a first phase in the development of the Orlando base. In September of 2002, the Frizen Missionary Training Center was dedicated.

The Church Partnerships Team

Pioneers Church Partnerships Team exists to move the local church and mission field closer together! Pioneers values partnership, and that is why we created the Church Partnerships Team (CPT). This team is the primary connection point between the local church and Pioneers. No church or agency can do missions alone. We want to learn how to better serve and assist the local church in mobilizing and developing people for effective service in missions.

Every partnership between a church and an agency has a different look and involves a lot of planning, communication and strong relationship building. Pioneers seeks to connect with churches in the following six ways:

- We facilitate and strengthen the church-agency partnership
- We help churches connect with their new appointees
- We host free Church Partner Forums for churches
- We encourage one-on-one consultations
- We foster relationships between field leadership and supporting churches
- We assist churches in sending out church-based teams

Partnering

Church Partner Forums are held twice yearly with the goal of strengthening the relationship between local churches and our agency. It is Pioneers desire to spend quality time in discussion with key church leaders, becoming better acquainted with each other and seeking the Lord for His vision with regard to our joint ministries in missions.

Facilitating Collaboration

One of the greatest strengths of our Church Partner Forums is the dialogue that can happen between like-minded church leaders as they come together to discuss the work of missions. Pioneers wants to be the catalyst for bringing together churches of differing size and in different stages of their commitment to missions, in order to spark ideas and forge new relationships furthering each church's calling to missions.

Fostering Relationships

Leaders of sending churches are consulted on major decisions involving their personnel in regards to relocation and major role changes. Most churches entrust the responsibility for the development of the ministry on the field to Pioneers. If a sending church desires to be more deeply involved in the ongoing decisions of the team on the field, a ministry agreement should be developed between the team, the Pioneers regional leader, the mobilization base, and the sending church.

Making Resources Available

A wealth of information is available in the "missions world" to help churches advance their global missions focus. Helping you connect to these tools is a way of serving that need. We can also help you network to other teams within the Orlando mobilization base.

Sending Out Church-based Teams

Pioneers encourages the leaders of sending churches to play an active role in preparing and recommending their missionaries for service, and in sustaining, encouraging and developing them throughout their ministry. We are committed to a team approach and welcome team-building with local churches for the mission field.

Purpose of This Handbook

Our passion as Church Partnerships Team members is to have a relationship with your church that will encourage and help you define your missions DNA.

This handbook has been designed to enable leaders of local churches to gain a perspective on the potential for partnering with Pioneers in the sending and support of missionaries. Together we desire to further a mutual goal to see God glorified among the unreached peoples of the world.

02 BASIC PRINCIPLES & PRACTICES

While the current operating structure of Pioneers has evolved over the years, several dominant themes continue to be reflected in the ministry of the mission. While each of these concepts is articulated in our mission statement and core values, several overarching principles can be identified and deserve special attention.

One important theme has been a combination of faith and flexibility that refuses to accept "closed doors." The gospel is to be preached, and churches planted, everywhere. This "can-do" attitude has inspired our missionaries with optimism and continues to unleash limitless creativity. Far-reaching fellowship policies are kept to a minimum, and authority and responsibility are decentralized to encourage creativity and initiative.

A second historical priority in Pioneers early development was unreached peoples. Our task was not to duplicate what others were doing, or to build on others' foundations, but to initiate church-planting movements in areas of greatest need and least opportunity to hear the gospel. This focus gave us a clear identity and biblical direction.

Pioneers has a strong desire to work with and assist Christian leaders of like vision around the world. The task of world evangelization belongs to the whole body of Christ, with each part helping the other, and all working in harmony. Thus, one of the significant activities of Pioneers is the support and encouragement of indigenous missionaries and church-planting movements.

The task of world evangelization belongs to the whole body of Christ.

Another distinctive of Pioneers is our eagerness to effectively involve the younger generation and tomorrow's leaders in the mission. Younger leaders are entrusted with significant responsibility. We enjoy a "high-trust/high-responsibility" fellowship environment that energizes our members. To sustain this we know that we have to trust God, to communicate openly with each other, and cannot allow the possibility of failure to keep us from pursuing our God-given goals.

All who serve the Lord with Pioneers are charged with the sacred trust of making prayer, worship, and the ministry of the Word their highest priority.

Pioneers desires to encourage and facilitate genuine cooperation between evangelical Christians worldwide in the planning, organizing, and implementing of our mission. Believing that this global vision is consistent with the biblical record and with the goal and nature of our task, Pioneers has committed itself to the pursuit of a global operational framework based on shared goals and values, and a common fellowship culture.

Mission Statement

Pioneers mobilizes teams to glorify God among unreached peoples by initiating church-planting movements in partnership with local churches.

Mission Statement Definitions

- "Unreached peoples" refers to ethno-linguistic people groups among whom there is no viable indigenous community of believing Christians with adequate numbers and resources to evangelize their own people without cross-cultural or other outside assistance.

- A "team" is a group of at least three missionary units (a unit is a couple or a single) who are committed to each other and to their common ministry task.

- A "church-planting movement" is a dynamic and self-perpetuating process of church multiplication, which may include a variety of ministry methods.

- "Partnership" refers to mobilization bases and the teams they serve, ministering in close cooperation with local churches both in the sending and receiving countries where possible. Pioneers personnel contribute as consultants, catalysts and equippers in the church-planting movement.

Core Values

Passion for God

Pioneers passion is to glorify God among the nations through obedience to the word of God, disciplined prayer, reliance on the Holy Spirit and worship. Pioneers strives to proclaim biblical truth, evidenced by integrity in lifestyle and relationships.

Unreached People Groups

Pioneers focuses on people groups with the greatest need and least opportunity to hear and understand the gospel.

Church-planting Movements

Pioneers initiates church-planting movements through evangelism and discipleship, resulting in dynamic, self-propagating churches with a missionary passion.

The Local Church

Pioneers partners with sending churches to mobilize and develop people for effective service. Pioneers teams endeavor to partner with national churches in their fields of ministry wherever possible.

Team Centered

Pioneers accomplishes its mission through teams mobilized from around the world. Teams develop and implement appropriate strategies using various gifts and methods while modeling Christian unity. Pioneers is committed to international fellowship, celebrating cultural diversity in the global task.

Innovation and Flexibility

Pioneers uses innovative means to gain access and minister effectively to unreached peoples. Pioneers is flexible and sensitive to the unique calling, vision and needs of each missionary.

Ethos of Grace

Pioneers affirms that God's grace operates uniquely in the lives of all believers. In all our relationships, we endeavor to cultivate an atmosphere of mutual acceptance and respect which encourages each of us to attain our full potential in Christ.

Participatory Servant Leadership

Pioneers empowers its members through a decentralized structure that emphasizes team-based servant-leadership and an interactive approach to decision making based on trust.

Ministry Methods

To fulfill the mission statement, Pioneers:

... mobilizes long-term missionaries from the international body of Christ. Short-term workers are also mobilized as appropriate.

... focuses on evangelism, discipleship, Bible teaching, church planting and leadership development among unreached peoples.

... uses innovative, relevant and culturally appropriate strategies.

... works in cooperation with others who share our evangelical position and purpose.

Statement of Faith

WE BELIEVE that the Holy Scriptures, consisting of Old and New Testaments, were originally given by God, divinely inspired, without error, infallible and are entirely trustworthy and the supreme authority in all matters of faith and practice.

WE BELIEVE in one God, Creator of all things, eternally existent in three persons: Father, Son and Holy Spirit.

WE BELIEVE in our Lord Jesus Christ, God manifest in the flesh, His virgin birth, sinless life, divine miracles, vicarious and atoning death on the cross, bodily resurrection, ascension and exaltation, mediatorial work, and personal, imminent and visible return in power and glory.

WE BELIEVE that Adam and Eve, created in the image of God, were tempted by Satan, the god of this world, and fell; that their sin has passed to all people, who as a result are lost, are unable to save themselves from the wrath of God, and need to be saved.

WE BELIEVE that salvation is a gift of God to those who repent and personally believe in Jesus Christ; that it is accomplished by God's grace through the shed blood of the Lord Jesus Christ and regeneration by the Holy Spirit.

WE BELIEVE in God the Holy Spirit who indwells all believers enabling them to live holy lives, and to witness and work for the Lord Jesus Christ despite opposition from the world, the flesh and Satan.

WE BELIEVE in the spiritual unity of all true believers, the universal Church, the body of Christ.

WE BELIEVE in the resurrection of both the saved and the lost; they that are saved unto the resurrection of eternal life with God, they that are lost unto the resurrection of eternal condemnation separated from God.

WE BELIEVE that Christ commanded the Church to go into all the world and make disciples of all peoples, baptizing them in the name of the Father, Son and Holy Spirit, and teaching those who believe to obey all that Christ commanded.

Guiding Grace Principles

Pioneers is an international fellowship comprised of evangelicals drawn from many different churches and backgrounds. Our desire is to work in harmony with our national church partners and Christian colleagues on the basis of essential doctrines as found in our statement of faith. These are doctrines on which, historically, there has been general agreement among all true followers of Christ.

In matters not addressed by our Statement of Faith, Pioneers acknowledges differing points of view provided they are based on the Bible as the supreme authority, and that no interpretation or practice will undermine the work of the gospel or the unity among those with whom we serve. We seek to live, work and relate to one another in a spirit of love and humility, as outlined in Romans 14, I Corinthians 13, and other passages.

International Organizational Structure

Pioneers has two core operational elements—mobilization bases and missionary teams. Pioneers' international leadership structure is comprised of the International Council (IC—for governance purposes), the International Director, and the International Leadership Team (ILT—providing international operational leadership). Each has clearly prescribed responsibilities and relate to one another in an atmosphere of mutual respect, influence and accountability.

Pioneers has an expanding network of missionary teams around the world. Each team is led by a team leader, and each team associates with other teams in their area. Team leaders in an area are served by and report to an area leader. Area leaders are served by and report to regional leaders, who report to the international director.

International Mobilization Bases

A mobilization base in partnership with local churches serves as the sending base for Pioneers missionaries from that country (or region). These missionaries are normally sent cross-culturally to serve on Pioneers teams.

A mobilization base partners with churches in the recruitment, preparation, appointment, care and servicing of its own Pioneers workers.

A mobilization base partners with churches in the recruitment, preparation, appointment, care and servicing of its own Pioneers workers. Each mobilization base is governed by a board, which provides legal and financial accountability. Each mobilization base is legally autonomous, and enters into ministry fellowship with other Pioneers mobilization bases according to mutually agreed standards. These standards are articulated in the international ministry agreement and the international handbook.

Candidates for missionary service apply to the mobilization base in their country of citizenship (or region) in accordance with the process established by that mobilization base. Each candidate must be in agreement with the statement of faith and core values of Pioneers and be willing to abide by the provisions of the international ministry agreement and international handbook.

The responsibilities of a mobilization base include:

- In partnership with churches, prayerfully mobilize (recruit, assess, train, appoint and assist) career and short-term missionaries for service with Pioneers.

- Provide quality service for personnel deployed by the mobilization base, including such services as handling financial affairs, member care, ongoing training, home assignment assistance and debriefing to those returning to their home country.

- Develop and maintain effective constituency relationships with churches, donors, training institutions and the Christian community.

- Develop and maintain a mobilization base handbook, containing all policies and procedures of particular relevance to Pioneers missionaries from that country.

- Participate actively in the International Council (IC) by sending delegates to Council meetings.

- Support financially the international operations of Pioneers.

- Prepare a semi-annual report for distribution to the international director, mobilization bases and International Leadership Team.

Currently active mobilization bases in addition to the U.S. are located in Ghana (Africa), Australia, Canada, Brazil (Latin America), United Kingdom (Europe), New Zealand, and Singapore (Southeast Asia).

03 THE TEAM APPROACH

The missionary team is the basic operational unit in Pioneers. The whole organization is structured to develop and facilitate effective teams.

Pioneers Concept of Teams

A team can be defined, simply, as a group of people who are committed to accomplishing a particular task in relationship with one another. In Pioneers, a team consists of three or more missionary "units." This may mean three singles, for example, or two couples and a single.

A true team effort can be distinguished by the extent to which people work together to accomplish the goal. This may not involve proximity, depending upon the ministry circumstances, but it does require interaction, both at the personal and professional level. Where depth of interaction can be increased (and frequency helps), the sense of teamwork will be enhanced.

A true team effort can be distinguished by the extent to which people work together to accomplish the goal.

Pioneers concept of teamwork involves the "total person." A missionary team is concerned for the development of each member's ministry and for the personal development of the worker. Members of a team encourage one another, stimulate one another, correct one another and pray regularly for one another. A team develops a life and culture of its own. Its members feel a strong sense of community and ownership over their "mission."

Role and Appointment of Team Coordinators

A new Pioneers team is started when God gives someone (a church or individual) a desire for a specific ministry (i.e. to reach a people group). Through a process of research and consultation with Pioneers regional and area leaders and their mobilization base, a decision is made as to whether a new team should be initiated. A key consideration involves leadership for the proposed team. Has God provided someone who can give initial leadership to the effort? If so, this person may become a "team coordinator." This appointment may occur while the new team coordinator is still in his/her sending country.

The leader of an emerging team is given team coordinator status until three ministry "units" (singles or couples) have arrived on the field as members of the team, and the area leader is satisfied that someone on the team has the necessary leadership capability to give ongoing oversight to the work. When these two criteria have been met, the area leader may appoint a team leader. This person may or may not be the same person who gave initial momentum to the work, depending on such factors as the gifting and ministry experience of the team members.

A team develops a life and culture of its own. Its members feel a strong sense of community and ownership over their mission.

While the role and responsibilities of a team coordinator are similar to that of a team leader, the emphasis is on getting the new ministry started. This involves research, communicating the vision, mobilizing prayer and recruiting workers for the emerging team, as well as providing overall leadership to the work in its early stages. The team coordinator will stay in regular touch with their area leader regarding the developing work. This is a period of closer interaction and mentoring.

Role and Appointment of Team Leaders

A Pioneers team leader is appointed by the area leader, in consultation with members of the team and after an appropriate reference from their mobilization base. Appointment is to a three-year renewable term. The appointment is ratified by the regional leader.

The team leader is responsible to provide oversight and leadership for the team. Their goal is to facilitate team life and decision-making with a view toward achieving maximum ministry fruitfulness of each member in the context of the team's ministry objectives.

A team leader must be conversant in English, and able to function within international leadership forums.

Accountability of Team Leaders and Coordinators

Team leaders and team coordinators, besides being accountable to their teams and to their support team, report to a Pioneers area leader. Standard reports must be submitted monthly. A personal/team ministry plan is submitted to the area leader at the conclusion of each year for the upcoming year.

Team leaders and team coordinators from a given area may meet from time-to-time for training and development in leadership, to discuss area and regional issues, share ideas and concerns, pray and fellowship together. This provides an additional source of peer-mentoring, accountability and encouragement.

Accountability of Team Members

Multiple lines of accountability can be identified in the routine life of a healthy team. First, each member is responsible to his/her sending church, support team and mobilization base. Second, other team members provide important input and are free to ask questions, providing a mutual accountability. Third, each member is formally accountable to the team leader. Each year the team member meets with the team leader to review personal growth and ministry progress of the previous year, and to discuss their goals for the coming year. A standard goal-setting format is used. Sending churches may receive a copy of this review upon request.

Where a team partners with national churches, individual members are accountable to the national church they serve, in accordance with whatever agreement or understanding governs their ministry relationship.

Role of the Area Leader

Area leaders provide leadership and oversight for the team leaders and team coordinators in a specified area. The area leader serves as a sounding board, a resource and mentor to team leaders. Generally the role of the area leader is to empower the team rather than to dictate decisions or strategy.

The area leader helps to develop leadership and strategy across a given geographic area for Pioneers (and with ideally no more than seven team leaders). He/she is on hand to help address special ministry or personnel problems that arise, and at times may need to mediate in conflicts or problems that the team leader/team coordinator has been unable to resolve.

Area leaders may organize area-wide or regional conferences or retreats from time-to-time, to bring together several teams for joint fellowship. They play an important coordinating and training role in communicating to and with teams in their areas, the regional leader and to mobilization bases on matters of importance that may affect missionaries. Area leaders are appointed by, and accountable to, a regional leader.

Role of the Regional Leader

Regional leaders provide oversight to area leaders and facilitate development of ministry vision for a broad geographic region. They provide a key link in international communication and the development of new ministries in the region. Pioneers currently has six regional leaders who are accountable to the international director.

Team Decision Making

Team decisions are normally made by consensus, as the members seek the will of the Lord together. Some well-established teams may ask new members to watch and listen for a few months before assuming full participation in team decision-making discussions.

Team leaders bear responsibility for the development of team members and the team's ministry. As such, team leaders are empowered to provide appropriate accountability and to make personnel-related decisions, and as needed, to gain counsel from their area leader.

Team decisions are normally made by consensus, as the members seek the will of the Lord together.

If a team member has serious reservations about the decision of the team leader or team, it is his/her responsibility to approach the team leader for private discussion of the matter. If the matter is not resolved after discussion and prayer, a written appeal may be made to the area leader, with a copy to the team leader. If there is still no resolution, a written appeal may be made to their regional leader with copies going to the team leader and area leader. In all communications, missionaries should be careful to honor the role and responsibility of the leadership. In situations not specifically addressed by mission policy, courtesy, spiritual wisdom and common sense should be applied.

Team members should make decisions on individual matters in light of the team's ministry strategy and objectives. At times, personal preferences will need to be set aside for the overall benefit and harmony of the team.

Team Ministry Strategy

An important mark of a healthy team is the development of an effective overall strategy to which the team is committed. This involves articulating a "mission statement" and agreeing to specific approaches and objectives for accomplishing it. The mission statement should be consistent with Pioneers broader mission statement. Strategies and ministries of the team should be carefully chosen in light of the overall goal. Individual members should contribute actively to the process of developing a team strategy, and evaluate their own ministry activities accordingly.

While a new team may have a preliminary strategy to work from in the early stages, it should be held lightly. A team needs time to learn the ministry context before establishing a detailed long-term plan. The early years should be spent laying a firm foundation.

Team Philosophy of Ministry

The team's philosophy of ministry will have less to do with specific activity and plans, and more to do with the why and how. A philosophy of ministry should address such things as the needs of the target group, an analysis of the history of efforts to reach them, a contextual ministry approach, the role of the missionary and the team's relationship to national churches.

Teams that do not take the time to discuss and document their philosophy and strategy may undermine their own potential for long-term fruitfulness.

Mutual Care and Accountability

Teams are the primary agent of "member care" on the field and are encouraged to foster caring relationships at various levels: 1) individual devotional disciplines 2) one-on-one accountability 3) family times and accountability 4) small group fellowship/study 5) team gatherings for various purposes.

Most teams will plan occasional retreats or workshops to supplement the needs of their members. Often, leaders from supporting churches are invited to minister to their missionaries on such occasions.

While the team is the primary source for member care on the field, the area leader is available as a resource person. Also, Pioneers has relationships with "specialists" who are available to visit teams on a routine basis to encourage and counsel missionaries, or to provide expert advice on ministry issues. Sending churches and mobilization bases are also alert to the needs of their personnel, and seek to provide ongoing care for them. Pioneers team members are encouraged to develop healthy relationships with people of other organizations.

04 THE MOBILIZATION PROCESS

The recruitment of a missionary prospect is a joint effort that involves the local church, missionary teams in the proposed field of service, and staff of the Pioneers mobilization base. This section seeks to define basic qualifications for missionary candidates, outline the steps in the recruiting process, and set forth the responsibilities of each of the participating groups in the mobilization of new personnel.

Designations of Personnel

We have adopted the following terms to help define the recruitment process of those we seek to mobilize:

- Inquirer: One who has expressed an initial interest in potential ministry with Pioneers.

- Applicant or Candidate: One who has applied to a Pioneers mobilization base but has not yet been formally accepted into membership.

- Edger: One who participates as a member of a Pioneers summer team.

- Appointee: One who has been appointed by a Pioneers mobilization base for missionary service and is preparing to join a team.

- Missionary: One who is engaged in a minimum of one year of field service with Pioneers.

- Mobilization Base Staff: One who serves with a Pioneers mobilization base.

General Candidate Qualifications

Anyone applying for a minimum of one year of service with Pioneers should (1) be a genuine believer of Jesus Christ as Lord and Savior, demonstrating spiritual maturity, the fruit of the Spirit and healthy interpersonal relationships; (2) give clear testimony to the call or leading of God to cross-cultural service; (3) be in agreement with Pioneers core documents (including the Statement of Faith); (4) have the approval and endorsement of a sending church; (5) demonstrate a knowledge of sound doctrine; (6) demonstrate one's commitment and ability through ministry experience; and (7) complete the candidate application process and orientation program outlined by the mobilization base (normally in the country of one's citizenship).

Pioneers handles each applicant individually; requirements vary depending on one's background, experience, and the anticipated field location and ministry role. Divorced candidates may be accepted. However, circumstances and reasons for the divorce, the timing of the divorce in relation to conversion, the involvement, if any, of children, financial obligations, the envisioned ministry role, and the attitude of the receiving national church and team are among the many factors taken into consideration before deciding upon the acceptability of the applicant for service with Pioneers.

As part of the process, the leadership of a divorced applicant's sending church is consulted prior to acceptance of the applicant. Appointment to a specific team cannot occur until the team leader has been informed of the situation in order to assess implications for ministry.

Role of Local Church

Most potential missionary candidates are the product of local churches with a solid emphasis on reaching the world with the message of Christ. Furthermore, the active church ministry of potential recruits is a key point of evaluation within the mobilization process. Pioneers especially values local churches who proactively encourage qualified members to consider and engage in cross-cultural ministry either in their own area of influence or overseas. Local church recommendation is required of all candidates and is

Most potential missionary candidates are the product of local churches with a solid emphasis on reaching the world with the message of Christ.

given the highest priority in consideration for appointment. The pastor's reference is an important gauge Pioneers uses to evaluate the relationship the Pioneers candidate has with their sending church.

Role of Missionary Team

Much of the responsibility for recruiting new workers rests with the missionary team. As a team develops its strategy, it begins to have an idea of how many workers will be needed and what skills or gifts may be required. All Pioneers team members should see themselves as mobilizers. Even when a team feels it has adequate personnel, its members should be alert for potential workers for other teams.

Each team is responsible to supply information that local churches and mobilization bases can use to attract and assist potential workers. At a minimum, some information of this type should be included in the team handbook, and a current team profile should be available.

The team leader should respond as promptly as possible to inquiries from mobilization bases and prospective candidates, furnishing whatever information is necessary. The process of carrying a candidate through from the point of initial inquiry to departure for the field is an interactive one, involving the individual, the sending church, the mobilization base and the team leader. As time for departure nears, a team leader will sometimes appoint a member of the team as a "point person" to answer the appointee's questions and "mentor" them during the early months of adjustment to the field.

Role of Mobilization Base

The mobilization base personnel recruit broadly and follow up with individual prospects. The mobilization base, in consultation with the prospective sending church and field leaders, also ensures that the candidate is adequately qualified, oriented and trained for the envisioned ministry. They encourage individuals through the process of preparation, whatever the time required.

Mobilizers are encouraged to correspond with appropriate field leaders at any time regarding prospective personnel and their possible field selection. Where mobilization bases and field leaders are both corresponding with a prospect, each should copy the other on any communication.

Mobilization bases generally have a periodic candidate orientation program, known as "Explore," for the purpose of orienting candidates to Pioneers as an organization. Anyone who appears to be a promising prospect for service on a Pioneers team may be invited to this orientation. Though the prospective missionary is under no obligation, as a general rule they come with an expectation to join Pioneers for the purpose of field service. This orientation is sometimes used by God as a final confirmation in the candidate's decision-making process.

Pioneers-USA presently holds eight orientation sessions each year.

Steps to Explore

Each missionary candidate is advised to follow these steps toward appointment for eventual service:

- Share and consult with local church leadership about their desire to pursue ministry and their interest in Pioneers. It is highly recommended that the appointee share their appointment letter with their sending church if they are offered and accept appointment.

- Complete a Start form which becomes a basis of initial evaluation and a platform for discussion with mobilization personnel.

- Complete the Application and distribute reference forms to be sent directly to Pioneers. A reference from the candidate's sending church leadership is required along with 3-6 personal references.

- Complete psychological tests and a doctrinal questionnaire for review prior to candidate orientation.

- Attend and participate in Explore.

Outcomes of Explore

At the end of the Explore week, Pioneers will indicate to the candidate that they qualify for one of the following categories:

- Appointee: Candidate is offered appointment. The appointment includes conditions that must be met during their pre-field period of ministry. The candidate can accept the appointment immediately or take up to a month to decide as they pray and consult with local church leadership and other mentors.

- Candidate-in-process: Candidates must fulfill conditions prior to being accepted as appointees.

- No appointment: Candidates in this category are not offered appointment.

Following Explore, final acceptance of an appointee to a specific team is the decision of the team leader.

05 PRE-FIELD CONSIDERATIONS

Pioneers recognizes the importance of appointee ministry prior to initially going to the mission field. Among the major facets of this ministry are personal preparation for field service, generating prayer and financial support, and maintaining an appropriate level of accountability to the appointee's sending church and to Pioneers. From the standpoint of the agency, this accountability relationship is facilitated through the pre-field coaches. The US mobilization base team is available to each appointee in their pre-field ministry.

Personal Preparation and Training

Each appointee will have specific needs in their preparation for effective service on the field. Pioneers seeks to help the appointee and the sending church define these needs based both on the background and experience of the appointee as well as their projected ministry and place of service. The customized program shared with each appointee at the conclusion of Explore will likely include several elements:

Bible Training

All appointees are required to complete the equivalent of 30 hours of Bible courses. For those who do not have 30 hours prior to application to Pioneers, typical requirements may include Old and New Testament survey, systematic theology, hermeneutics and world missions. These requirements may be completed within the first five years after their appointment date, provided that significant progress is made each year toward that goal.

Pre-field Language Training

Language acquisition skills can be significantly enhanced through participation in one of a number of programs currently available at several centers within the United States.

Cross-cultural Training

Appointees who are limited in their cross-cultural experience may be asked to enhance their background in this area through participating in courses such as cultural orientation or more specific offerings such as Islamic, Hindu or Buddhist studies.

Local Church Ministry Experience

Pioneers places a priority on the need for all appointees to have significant ministry experience in a local church. This background is vital to effective church planting overseas. Whenever possible, if training of this type is required, we desire that it be facilitated through the sending church.

Launch (Pre-field Training)

This is a week-long program held at least five times a year. This program is required for appointees who anticipate leaving for the field within the next six months to a year. It is a time of reconnecting with US mobilization base team members, training in team and personal development, introduction to church planting, discussing field specific issues and preparing for the changes ahead. There is also a program for children to help them prepare for the life-changes they will face.

Generating Prayer and Financial Support

Pioneers appointees have the responsibility of sharing the vision God has given them and of allowing Him to raise up those whom He has chosen to support the ministry. We encourage each appointee to maintain their confidence in the God who has called them and to approach this responsibility without apology. By the same token, we seek to help them plan and organize their efforts in a manner consistent with what we believe are sound biblical principles. To this end we encourage them in these areas:

Relating to Sending Church

All appointees are reminded that they are to *serve* their sending church in any way the church leadership sees fit. They can significantly help the church to be more effective in its missionary outreach. In this context we encourage appointees to meet with pastors and/or missions committees, share their vision and specific plan for ministry, seek prayer support and discuss their financial needs. These activities should be carried out in a spirit of submission to counsel and policies of the sending church.

Enlisting Other Churches

In addition to a primary sending church, appointees are encouraged to contact other churches to become part of their ministry team. Sending churches should be responsive to this need and can also help facilitate these contacts.

Individual Contacts

In addition to family and close friends who are committed to the appointee, other people will often make up an important part of a missionary support team. Appointees are encouraged to cultivate these contacts and view them as a significant opportunity for ministry.

Accountability to Sending Church

The sending church is vital to the pre-field ministry of Pioneers appointees. Not only do we expect appointees to hold membership in the church, we emphasize their need to view the church as playing the key role in their entire pre-field ministry. Appointees are thus accountable to their sending church. Sending churches are encouraged to develop a defined structure for maintaining this relationship and

Appointees are accountable to their sending church, and sending churches are encouraged to develop a defined structure for maintaining this relationship.

to communicate frankly and openly their expectations to the appointees.

Pioneers and the Sending Church

Pioneers desires to come alongside churches and work together. Partnership is one of Pioneers' core values. A question churches and candidates often ask is: "What does it mean to be a sending church in partnership with Pioneers?"

The Sending Church as a Partner with Pioneers

1. A sending church is a fellowship of believers that identifies potential cross-cultural workers within its fellowship and gives witness to their character, call, experience, and giftedness.

2. A sending church embraces its primary role of spiritual authority and care.

3. A sending church strives to be a catalyst in the preparation, training, care, and funding of its worker.

4. A sending church acknowledges the empowerment and calling of the Holy Spirit for the commissioning and releasing of their worker to field of service.

5. A sending church participates in partnership with Pioneers to work on teams among the unreached.

6. A sending church faithfully prays for fruitful ministry among its worker's unreached people group.

Pioneers as a Partner with the Sending Church

1. Pioneers exists to partner with the sending church to send cross-cultural workers who initiate church-planting-movements among unreached peoples.

2. Pioneers provides accountability and care in financial, personal, and spiritual matters.

3. Pioneers assists the sending church with recruitment, evaluation, preparation, and care of cross-cultural workers.

4. Pioneers responds to the unique shape God has give each sending church, and assists it to develop and

sustain vision for its ministry among the unreached.

5. Pioneers pursues pathways for expanding the ministry of the sending church in cross-cultural contexts.

6. Pioneers faithfully prays for sending churches in their pursuit of God's heart for the nations.

Sending Church Relationship Acknowledgement Form

PIONEERS	Relationship to your Sending Church Agreement and Authorization	Initials

From its inception, PIONEERS has recognized the vital importance of the role of the Sending Church in the life and ministry of the PIONEERS Field Member. Partnership with the Local Church remains a core value of PIONEERS.

As a Field Member of PIONEERS USA, I recognize and affirm the importance of my relationship to my Sending Church. Harvey Lane Baptist Church , at 210 Shoemaker Way, Hackleton, NJ 21145 , (444-342-5785) is my Sending Church who has "set me apart"/ commissioned, and assigned me to PIONEERS USA as a minister of Jesus Christ to serve in cross cultural missions.

	WC	DC

I recognize and accept that membership and employment with PIONEERS USA is conditioned on my acceptance and consent to the following terms that describe and define my relationship with, and PIONEERS USA's relationship with my Sending Church:

	WC	DC

As an Appointee—Prior to departure for the field or active involvement in ministry with PIONEERS, I agree to complete all requirements of my Sending Church. I will work to establish healthy structures to maintain my relationship with my Sending Church, establish commonly agreed upon communication practices and openly discuss expectations. I recognize and accept that my Sending Church must give approval for my specific field assignment, and must formally "set me apart"/commission me to serve under the direction of PIONEERS USA.

	WC	DC

As a Field Member in Active Service with PIONEERS—While day-to-day decisions are made on the field and immediate accountability lies with my field leadership, I accept my responsibility to keep my Sending Church informed about my and my family's well-being and ministry, as well as invite my Sending Church leadership into decisions pertaining to my on-going service and assignment. This includes significant changes in ministry or relocation, a change in role or life status, a request for Extended or Special Leave, and any urgent or challenging situation that may require significant member care or impact my ability to minister.

	WC	DC

I give my consent and authorize PIONEERS leadership, including my field leaders and leadership of the US Mobilization Base, at their discretion, to consult with the authorized leadership of my Sending Church as identified below regarding any of the issues as described in the above paragraph.

	WC	DC

I recognize that PIONEERS USA reserves the sole right and authority to determine my membership and employment status with the Mission, and though my Sending Church will normally be consulted, the final decision regarding any necessary disciplinary or restorative measures that could affect my ongoing membership/employment with the Mission belongs to PIONEERS USA alone.

	WC	DC

I release PIONEERS and its staff from all liability arising out of the use and exchange of any information covered by this Authorization. This includes, but is not limited to, all statutory and legal claims of defamation, invasion of privacy and breach of confidentiality.

	WC	DC

	Member Signature	Member Spouse Signature (if applicable)	Date
Print Name	William Carey	Doroth	

NOTE: After appointment PI members (husband & wife) will be asked to fill out, initial and sign this document which will then be sent to the listed Authorized Church leaders to sign electronically.

	Signature of Authorized Church Leader	Signa	
Print Name	John Ryland	Date:	And
Role:	Sr. Pastor		Missions Pastor
Email:	Ryland@mmail.com		Fuller@mmail.com

There are two reasons we use the Relationship to Your Sending Church Agreement and Authorization Form:

1. Pioneers recognizes the important spiritual role of the sending church in the life and ministry of our field workers and appointees. We acknowledge the spiritual accountability and authority that comes when a church commissions and sends their own into global missions. We also realize that practical realities must be considered in any partnership involving shared ministry in missions. Our desire is to see that the local church is included and respected in this process of sending people to the field. This partnership between Pioneers and the Sending Church is a unique shared opportunity to uphold the missionary in a supportive way and come alongside when the need arises. This form clarifies both for the Field Member and the Sending Church leadership the key points of expectation in regard to the Field Member's relationship with their Sending Church and that of Pioneers' relationship to their Sending Church as it concerns their Field Member. It is very important for us to establish a clear understanding and agreement regarding communication between PI leadership and your Sending Church leadership for matters that may arise as you minister as a member of Pioneers.

2. Pioneers does not have "church" or "religious order" status with the government, and therefore we look to the field member's Sending Church to be the entity recognized by the government as authorized to "set apart" or "commission" individuals for ministry, and who assigns their "set apart" missionary/minister to Pioneers for mission work. In this respect, when it comes to employment regulations, we may consider our Field Members to be "ministers". This form assists us to reinforce this understanding.

Accountability to Pioneers

Appointee accountability to Pioneers has as its goal the timely departure of each appointee for their field of service after having fulfilled all pre-field requirements. This accountability is exercised through the pre-field coaches who provide encouragement and assistance throughout the process.

Most appointees make steady progress towards the field by taking steps to complete their pre-field ministry responsibilities. They usually will take between six months and three years to reach the field once they have been appointed. The following guidelines have been established to help appointees and sending churches understand how Pioneers program of appointee accountability works and how their progress will be evaluated.

An appointee's progress is evaluated quarterly by their pre-field coaches from their date of appointment after Explore until they reach the field.

If the appointee is not making definite progress towards the field, their situation will be carefully reviewed, and in some cases an inactive status will be recommended.

Definition of Inactive Status

For reasons of health, indebtedness, re-evaluating the future, failure to complete quarterly reports, etc., an appointee may be temporarily "inactive" in regard to pursuing service overseas. An appointee can request inactive status by contacting the pre-field coaches, or an appointee may be asked to move to this status according to the appointee accountability guidelines. Appointees on inactive status cannot draw funds from their accounts.

An appointee on inactive status will be required to be interviewed by the pre-field coach when they are once again ready to move in the direction of field service. An appointee who has resigned from Pioneers may be reinstated again into the mission, but only after completing the normally required steps of candidate appointment.

06 MEMBER CARE

Member care is a growing field of service to missionaries to encourage them to be all they can be for God and to empower them to attain their God-given goals and objectives in ministry. It includes aspects of comfort, encouragement, listening, challenge, accountability, exhortation, correction and confrontation. At times it resembles counseling, training, pastoral care, discipleship, human resources, and/or friendship. The Member Development Team within the Orlando mobilization base coordinates member care for Pioneers-USA. The responsibility is shared at various times with the sending church, the missionary team, the team leader, area leader and others. The best member care is provided when field leadership, sending church leadership and the Member Development Team are all actively engaged in the process.

The Scope of Member Care

Pioneers is committed to the establishment of church-planting teams among unreached peoples. Most of the remaining unreached people groups live in "restricted access" areas. Long-term church planting among such groups requires a strong and determined missionary. Pioneers understands that the tremendous challenges on the field inevitably will stress the staying power of many of our people. Member care involves supporting these missionaries in a way that will allow them to serve effectively under highly adverse conditions and avoid undesirable levels of missionary attrition.

The following are some examples of member care concerns that can occur with our cross-cultural workers:

- Difficulty adjusting to the new culture overseas
- Political, medical or personal crises
- Mental health conditions like anxiety or depression which develop overseas
- Feeling discouraged, isolated or lonely
- Interpersonal or ministry conflict with teammates or leadership
- Lack of fulfillment in ministry
- Difficulty learning a language
- Spiritual warfare
- Adjustment of children, especially teenagers
- Educational needs of children
- Transition to a new team or ministry
- Re-entry and/or repatriation of the missionary
- Personal sin

Member Development Team

Pioneers Member Development Team exists "to champion growth and renewal in Pioneers members." It is staffed by a team leader and multiple member development consultants, some with particular specialties like counseling, spiritual formation, debriefing, third culture kids, hospitality, connecting with retirees, etc. Church leaders are encouraged to communicate at any time with the Member Development Team.

While a missionary is serving overseas, field leadership takes primary responsibility for the care of each missionary, with the sending church and Member Development taking a secondary role. When the missionary returns to the US, the sending church and Member Development Team assume primary responsibility for the missionary with field leadership taking a secondary role. Again, member care is best delivered when the sending church, field leadership and Member Development Team are in good communication throughout all phases of the missionary journey.

Member care is best delivered when the sending church, field leadership and Member Development Team are in good communication.

In response to the member care needs of our missionaries, the Member Development Team serves in the following ways, among others:

- A personal debrief is offered to all missionaries on home assignment.

- When any crisis of personnel develops, Member Development engages field leadership, the sending church and the missionary to manage and respond to the crisis or situation.

- CONNECT, our four- day group debriefing retreat, is offered twice a year. This retreat helps missionaries to connect with God, others and themselves.

- Counseling assessment and referrals are managed for those who need professional counseling.

- Direct communication with missionaries to encourage, dialogue or engage with them on an issue of importance to them.

- Information management and human resources function, i.e. the member development team manages the database on our missionaries, keeps personnel and medical files, tracks leave time, etc.

- Trips to the field during conferences for the purpose of consulting with field leaders and directly caring for missionaries. A representative is sent to every conference held overseas.

- A specialized focus on missionary children. Aspects of this program include: prefield training, kids programs at conferences, a newsletter, education seminar, debriefing for children and a college scholarship fund.

- Help for missionaries transitioning out of Pioneers in the form of career assessment, debriefing, encouragement and communicating with support constituency.

- Resources are provided on topics of relevance to missionaries—books, publications, web sites, DVDs, etc.

Member Care: A Shared Responsibility

The local church is a key partner in supporting missionaries throughout their missionary journey. While the person responsible for the care of missionaries within the organization changes over their missionary journey, the sending church remains constantly involved throughout the span of their service.

Pioneers views it as the responsibility of the missionary to stay in touch with the sending church. Sending churches are encouraged to communicate regularly with their missionary and care for them in any and every way they are able to. When things are going well for a particular missionary, there will likely not be a lot of direct communication from Pioneers to the sending church, although communication is always encouraged. The sending church is invited to request feedback at any time on their missionary and/or give feedback to Pioneers on how we may best serve them.

When an urgent or challenging situation with a missionary develops, Pioneers will contact the sending church to bring them in on the issue, and seek their input on the way forward. The sending church is considered to be included in the circle of confidentiality regarding issues or concerns about their missionary.

07 FINANCIAL CONSIDERATIONS

This section is intended to assist partner churches of Pioneers in understanding the financial policies of the mission. The overall financial philosophy is intended to balance the necessity of compliance with all governmental regulations regarding tax-exempt organizations with the desire to see each worker reach their full potential for ministry. An appropriate level of financial accountability is essential, not just to maintain a good relationship before God, but also to demonstrate good stewardship to our partner churches and donors.

> **Financial accountability is essential, not just to maintain a good relationship before God, but to demonstrate good stewardship to our partner churches and donors.**

In addition to being accountable to God as good stewards of His provision, Pioneers mobilization bases have a legal obligation to governmental agencies to account for funds received. Tax-deductible donations must be used in a manner consistent with Pioneers-USA non-profit objectives as filed with the IRS (evangelization of unreached people groups, church planting, etc.). This obligation extends to each individual missionary unit. Therefore, Pioneers-USA financial policies are formed to ensure proper accountability standards with the government on both a mission-wide and individual level. An independent CPA firm audits us annually. A copy of Pioneers audit is available for download at www. pioneers.org.

Contributions and Support Raising: General Guidelines

For contributions to be tax-deductible, they must be made to Pioneers and not to specific individuals. It is important that donors understand that they are making a contribution to Pioneers who must control the funds after they are donated. Pioneers will, in turn, seek to fully honor the request of donors in using such funds for the intended ministry purpose. In communicating with donors or potential donors, we encourage missionaries and appointees to use terms such as:

- Pray that God would provide the support I need to raise for Pioneers.
- Thank you for your prayers and financial gifts to Pioneers.
- As you know, 100% of our salary comes from Pioneers and is made possible through generous donations of people who support Pioneers.
- I need to form a team of ministry partners who will support Pioneers with monthly financial commitments and prayer.
- Thanks for making Pioneers ministry around the world possible.
- God has provided 50% of the support I need to raise for Pioneers.
- Please continue to pray for the Pioneers ministry team I'm responsible to develop.

Tax-deductible receipts are sent for all valid donations and all donors, whether churches or individuals, should receive them within two to three weeks from when they sent the donation. Donors should contact our office at (407) 382-6000 if no receipt has been received within a month. Pioneers does not send reminders (bills) to donors whose pledges have lapsed. A return portion is included with each receipt for the donor to use for their next donation and contains all the information needed for the Finance

Team to properly credit an account with future donations. It is the missionary's responsibility to track donors' giving. Software is available at no charge that will also assist the missionary in tracking donor giving.

Missionaries/Appointees are NOT allowed to raise funds specifically for personal items such as home schooling, personally owned vehicles, vacations, household items, etc. Checks marked clearly as non-tax deductible personal gifts (birthdays, Christmas, etc.) from individuals may be received by Pioneers on behalf of appointees and field workers. These gifts are forwarded in full to the individual as intended by the donor. If a receipt is issued, it will be marked "non-deductible." Pioneers does not allow churches to give "personal" gifts to its missionaries through the mission.

Missionary Accounts and Administrative Fees

Pioneers maintains two accounts for each appointee and missionary. The departure account is used to accumulate contributions that have specifically been intended for one-time outgoing expenses. These contributions are only available for expenses related to departure for the overseas field. Once the appointee has left for foreign service, any remaining balance is transferred to their support account.

The support account is the source of both salary and expense reimbursement and is the place where most regular financial activity takes place.

All appointees and field workers are assessed an administrative fee known as a "service fee." Service fees provide approximately 40% of Pioneers-USA's headquarters expenses, including missionary oversight and care, financial services, recruiting and maintaining headquarters facilities. The support of the headquarters breaks down as follows:

- Direct contributions and grants (13%)
- US mobilization base team support income raised directly (34%)
- Service fees (42%)

- Training fees, interest, sales, accommodations (11%)

A service fee of 10% is assessed on all contributions. Once field service begins, the assessment is a minimum of $150 a month for singles and $250 per married couple, and a maximum of $400 per month for singles and $650 per month for married couples.

There is also a service fee of 2% on all missionary support toward the cost of essential international leadership and ministry services of Pioneers, which is placed in the "International Fund." This fee applies only to field missionaries' support and not to appointees or projects. The minimum is $30 per month for singles (maximum of $80) and $50 per month for married couples (maximum of $130).

Pre-Field Allowances

Appointees may be reimbursed for expenses incurred during pre-field ministry. Examples of allowable expenses include ministry-related travel costs, printing and postage expense and telephone, fax and email transmission charges. Some training expenses are also allowable.

No education expenses leading to a degree or Bible certificate prior to full-time overseas service are reimbursable since such education qualifies the missionary for a new trade. Education expenses, which are not tax-deductible, cannot be paid (as either ministry expenses OR salary) using tax-exempt donations. Some training is deductible such as cross-cultural, linguistics or language schools, provided the employee have first met the minimum educational requirements of Pioneers, or if they are working full-time on the field.

The following rules and guidelines are provided for the purpose of determining whether or not expenses in the U.S. for education are deductible.

1.   Ordinary and necessary expenses are deductible/reimbursable, even though the education may lead to a degree, if it:

- is required for keeping a salary, status or job, or

- maintains or improves skills required in doing present work. This includes refresher courses or courses dealing with current developments, as well as academic or vocational courses.

2. Education expenses are considered personal, and therefore non-deductible/reimbursable, if the education is:

- required in order to meet the minimum educational requirements to qualify a person for a job (such as Pioneers minimum 30 hours of Bible training requirement), or

- part of a program of study that will lead to qualifying a person for a new trade or business (such as going to seminary for an M.Div. degree before leaving for the field). A change of duties is not considered a new trade or business if the new duties involve the same general work presently done.

3. Educational expenses include amounts spent for tuition, books, supplies, laboratory fees, correspondence courses, tutoring costs, research, typing of papers and similar items. If travel away from home is necessary to obtain education for which expenses are reimbursable, expenses for travel, meals, and lodging are also valid expenses.

A salary may be sent to the appointee monthly, up to the maximum salary allowance determined by the director of finance. The amount of salary paid during deputation is based on the level of active ministry that furthers the tax-exempt purpose of Pioneers. Fund-raising for future ministry qualifies as active ministry, but going to school does not. As a general rule, appointees may not receive a salary until a few months before their anticipated departure.

Support Schedule

During candidate orientation, appointees receive a specific support schedule for their targeted field. The support schedule is estimated for each missionary unit, based on financial requirements set jointly by

During candidate orientation, appointees receive a specific support schedule for their targeted field.

the Vice-President of Finance and the team leader for the appointed field, with adjustments made for particular needs within maximum limits. One hundred percent of the minimum support figure set MUST be raised before going to the field, and the team leader must give permission to arrive on the field at less than the recommended amount of support.

The support schedule is broken down into three basic categories: 1) Personal (Taxable) Expenses, 2) Ministry (Non-taxable) Expenses, and 3) Departure Expenses.

Personal expenses include items that are considered taxable by the IRS and include the following:

Personal Allowance is the figure set for day-to-day living expenses while on the field. This amount includes food, clothing, tithe and personal transportation.

Regarding unpaid school loans, Pioneers allows appointees to depart before repaying them only if the repayment of such loans can be handled through existing support levels. Finance will handle these payments as part of the personal allowance.

Children's allowance is given on the support schedule for each dependent child in the family and will vary according to cost of living on each field. It normally takes into account changes in needs, as the children get older. IRS rules for dependency apply to determining whether a child can be claimed for support schedule purposes.

Children's education includes amounts spent for home schooling or other private education. It would include tuition, mandatory fees and travel to a distant school if necessary. The amount is based upon individual and field-based circumstances and is always subject to the availability of funds.

An allowance for college-aged children may also be received by the parents as long as the child is a full-time student.

Social Security/self-employment tax is the federal withholding Pioneers deposits monthly to cover self-employment tax liability (Social Security for ordained/

licensed ministers) on total taxable income. If the missionary is not ordained, this line would be for Social Security taxes Pioneers withholds as the employer.

Retirement: Pioneers requires that all workers going to the field make some provision for retirement. Pioneers works with Financial Management Network Inc. (FMN) to provide a voluntary tax deferred or after tax salary reduction plan. In most cases, we recommend putting retirement funds in a Roth 403(b).

Life insurance: All overseas workers and appointees on deputation who are paid a full-time salary are automatically covered for $10,000 ($5,000 additional for spouses and $2,000 for each child) by a group life insurance policy which comes with the Pioneers-sponsored health insurance plan.

However, families are required to purchase additional life insurance so that the total face value of all policies is at least $100,000. (Single workers do not have to purchase a life insurance policy unless someone else is dependent on their income.) The recommended level for a married male with two or more young children is at least $200,000 of term life insurance.

Ministry expenses are those items that the IRS allows us to reimburse to the missionary as a tax free reimbursement assuming the proper documentation has been submitted. These include the following:

- Work funds reimburse individual ministry expenses while on the field.

- Field travel is ministry-related non-personal travel while the missionary is active at their field of service.

- Training/education provides funds for language learning after arrival on the field.

- Postage/printing supports the cost of prayer letters and other ministry-related correspondence.

- Home assignment travel is withdrawn monthly and placed in a separate account reserved for furlough-related expenses. It is only available when tickets home are purchased.

- Health insurance is automatically transferred from field missionary accounts as a deductible ministry expense.
- Team transfers are administrative expenses which are required at the option of the team. They may be used for a variety of purposes, including the cost of team or area retreats.

Departure Requirements Include the Following:

Initial personal allowance: A departure support schedule allows the appointee to take at least one month's salary to meet personal needs until the first regular monthly remittance arrives on the field.

Training and rent deposit: Certain areas require a pre-payment of one semester's tuition for language learning. Others may require a significant down payment for rent as much as one to three years in advance.

Shipping: Most departure support schedules will include an amount for shipping items overseas to the field. This figure also includes any customs duties assessed en route, as well as charges for overweight baggage.

Equipment, outfit, and home set-up: Provision is made for expenses related to beginning a new ministry and setting up a new home.

Only those items directly related to ministry can be paid/reimbursed on a "non-taxable" basis. These items will remain Pioneers property indefinitely. If they are sold, the funds must be redeposited, or a statement must be submitted outlining the disposition of the funds. Items related to setting up a home, except for ministry office, and any other personal items purchased with departure funds, must be listed as taxable income earned.

Vehicle: Some fields may recommend raising funds for a vehicle before leaving for the field. Often this is optional and may be delayed until after arrival overseas.

Requests for Support Level Information

Churches frequently inquire about a missionary's support level. Typically, a request will ask for "support needed" and "support income received." Our response to these two questions is to communicate the "recommended" support level for the missionary. Since Pioneers utilizes ranges for support levels, this amount may be more or less than what the missionary is currently receiving. We calculate "support income received" as the 12-month average (after removing large one-time or special purpose gifts). Please contact the missionary for "committed monthly support" amounts, as the Finance Team does not update that information once the missionary has moved overseas. The "committed" amount may differ substantially from the 12-month average of what is actually received.

Church Communication with Pioneers Finance Team

Pioneers encourages churches to communicate with the Finance Team on issues of mutual interest. Good communication enables us to better serve you. The following guidelines will help improve this communication process.

Please send only finance related questions to the Finance Team. Please do not assume that finance questions sent to another team will be forwarded on to Finance or vice versa.

Pioneers encourages churches to communicate with the Finance Team on issues of mutual interest. Good communication enables us to better serve you.

Mail: If you are mailing correspondence to Pioneers for the Finance Team, please write "Finance Team" on the envelope. This makes it easier for the individual sorting the mail and assures that your communication will end up on the right desk.

E-mail: The church contact e-mail address for Finance is dollars@orlandoteam.com. If you have a question for Finance, this address will ensure that your communication is forwarded to the appropriate individual within the team. Please be sure to include a phone number where you can be reached in case further follow-up is needed. You may also contact members of the Finance Team directly at their individual e-mail addresses.

Fax: Pioneers fax number is (407) 382-1008. If you are faxing the Finance Team, please include "Attn: Finance" on your cover sheet to ensure that it is routed properly for prompt handling.

WE WANT TO HEAR FROM YOU

While Pioneers' U.S. Mobilization Base staff includes people with a wide variety of responsibilities, the Church Partnerships Team has as its objective to strengthen relationships between Pioneers and sending and supporting churches. This team was formed to serve as a point of personal connection to Pioneers. Members of our team would love to hear from you and come alongside you.

Learn more or connect with the Church Partnerships Facilitator who serves your region by visiting *Pioneers.org/ Send/ChurchPartners* or contacting Denny Spitters, VP of Church Partnerships, at 407-581-7317. We're listening!